THIS IS A CARLTON BOOK

Text, illustrations, design copyright
© Carlton Books Limited

Published in 2007 by
Carlton Books Limited
20 Mortimer Street
London W1T 3JW

10 9 8 7 6 5 4 3 2 1

A CIP catalogue record for this book is
available from the British Library

ISBN 978-1-84442-055-1

executive editor: **Lisa Dyer**

managing art director: **Lucy Coley**

editor: **Lara Maiklem**

design: **Barbara Zuñiga**

production: **Ed Carter**

illustrator: **Anna Hymas**

Printed and bound in Great Britain

Rude Jokes for Bad Girls

CARLTON
BOOKS

CONTENTS

HOW
COME?

How do we know God is a man?

If God was a woman she'd have made sperm chocolate-flavoured.

Why did Moses wander in the desert for 40 years?

Because even back then men wouldn't ask for directions.

Why do we call it
an 'orgasm'?
**Because it's easier to
spell than 'Uh-uh-uh-oh-
oh-oh-o-o-eeeeeeeee!!!'**

**What do you call ten naked guys sitting
on each other's shoulders?**

A scrotum pole!

Why do doctors slap
babies' bums when they're born?
**To knock the dicks
off the clever ones.**

Why is a blonde
like a good bar?
**Liquor in the front,
poker in the rear.**

Why don't men often show their true feelings?

They don't have any.

Did you hear about the baby that was born half male and half female?

It had a penis and a brain.

What's the scientific name for a female-to-male sex change?

A Strapadicktome.

Why doesn't a woman have the brain of a man?

Because she doesn't have a dick to keep it in.

Boys, what do you get if you cross your girlfriend with a pit-bull?

Your very last blowjob!

How do you get a pound of meat out of a fly?

Unzip it.

What happened when the chef got his hand caught in the dishwasher?
They both got fired.

What's the difference between a boyfriend and a husband?

About 35 minutes.

What do you call an intelligent, good-looking, sensitive man?

A rumour.

What's a man's idea of safe sex?

A padded headboard.

How can you tell if a man has manners?

He gets out of the bath to take a pee.

Why are men like spray paint?

One squeeze and they're all over you!

Why are men like
disposable tissues?
**You can pick them up,
blow them and then toss
them aside.**

**What's short and gets
straight to the point?**
A nymphomaniac midget.

What's the difference between
'Ooooh' and 'Aaahhh!!'?
About three inches.

**How do you get a man to stop giving
you oral sex?**
Marry him.

**What's the difference between love, true
love, and showing off?**
Spitting, swallowing, and gargling.

What do you do if your boyfriend walks out on you?

Shut the door!

Why is casual sex so great?

You don't have to wear heels.

How do you give a dog a bone?

Tickle his balls.

Why does a honeymoon only last seven days?

Because seven days makes a whole week.

What did the Irish spinster always say in her prayer?

'Dear Lord, please have Murphy on me...'

Which two things in the air can get a girl pregnant?

Her feet!

Why can't Stevie Wonder sort his laundry?

He's a man.

What do you call a man with a one-inch dick?

Justin.

Why do men die before women?

Who cares?

BOYS WILL
BE BOYS

A man walks into a chemist's owned by a couple of old ladies. **'I have a problem with my penis,' he tells them.** 'It's ten inches long and always stays hard, even after having sex for hours at a time. What can you give me for it?' The spinsters whisper to each other. Eventually they come to a decision. One says, **'The best we can offer you is £400 a week and a third interest in the store.'**

Little **Suzie** tells her friend that her dad has **two dicks.** 'That's impossible,' says the friend. 'No it's not,' says Suzie. 'I've seen them.' 'So what do they look like?' asks the friend. Suzie says, 'One's small, white and floppy, and he uses it for peeing. **And the other's long, stiff and pink, and he uses it for brushing mummy's teeth.'**

Size Chart

9 inches	Oh shit, owch!
7 inches	Oh yes, mmm!
6 inches	That'll do nicely thank you!
5 inches	Mmm, yeah ok!
4 inches	Could you try pushing a little more!
3 inches	Is it in yet?
2 inches	Oh forget it! Just use your tongue.

A man goes to see his doctor. **'My dick has holes all up and down the sides,'** he says. 'When I go to the toilet it sprays out everywhere. Can you help me?' The doctor looks at the man's perforated dick and hands him a business card. 'Is this a specialist?' asks the man. 'No,' says the doctor. 'We can't cure it. But the guy on the card is a clarinet tutor – **he can teach you how to hold it.'**

What is the difference between men and pigs?

**Pigs don't turn into men
when they drink.**

What do a clitoris, a birthday, and a toilet bowl all have in common?
Men usually miss them.

What's the average guy's idea of foreplay?

Half-an-hour of begging.

What do you call a guy whose missing 95% of his brain?
Castrated.

As the result of a **surgical mix-up**, a female brain cell happens to end up in a man's head. The brain cell looks around inside the skull – the place seems deserted. 'Hello!' she shouts. 'Is there anyone here?' There's no answer, so the brain cell shout out louder. 'Hello!! Is anyone there???' Suddenly she hears a faint voice calling up from the man's crotch. **'Hi! We're all down here... !'**

Ten Things You Probably Shouldn't Say To A Naked Man

1   Oh! Never mind! I think they have surgery to fix that.

2   My brother has one just the same. He's five years old.

3   Well, this explains your car...

4 Stay there! I'll get my tweezers.

5 Hey! Isn't there a tower in Italy like that?

6 Was your dad a pygmy?

7 Did you ever date Lorena Bobbitt?

8 Is it that cold in here?

9 Is that some sort of optical illusion?

10 Okay. So where did you put the rest of it?

Men and women have different views about sex and relationships: women want a relationship without the complication of unnecessary sex; men want sex without the complication of an unnecessary relationship.

A man goes to a doctor with an **orange dick**. 'That's extraordinary,' says the doctor. 'Do you work with dyes or other chemicals?' 'No,' says the man. 'Do you work near radioactivity?' asks the doctor. 'No,' says the man. 'I don't work at all. I'm on the dole.' 'So what do you do all day?' asks the doctor. The man replies, 'Mostly I sit on the sofa **watching porn** and eating **Cheesy Wotsits**.'

What's the quickest way to a man's heart? Through his rib cage.

Definition of a man: **a life-support machine for a dick.**

What's the main difference between men and women?

A woman wants one man

to satisfy her every need;

a man wants every woman

to satisfy his one need.

**What makes men
chase women they have
no intention of marrying?**
The same urge that makes dog chase
vehicles they have no intention of driving.

The government has just announced
it will be introducing a penis tax
**– the only tax men will
willingly overpay**.

A religious man wants to find a 'pure' woman to marry, so he invents a test to see how much his dates know about sex – when he's next out with a girl he'll show her his dick and see how she responds. On his next date, the man suddenly whips out his dick out and says, 'What's that?' The shocked woman says, **'That's a cock.'** 'You Jezebel!' says the man. 'If you were pure you wouldn't know what to call it.' The next week he goes on a date with another woman and, again, whips out his dick. 'What's that?' he says. The blushing woman responds, **'Well, I'd call it a penis.'** 'Hah!' says the man. 'If you were pure you wouldn't know what it was, you harlot.' The man goes on yet another date, but this time when he whips out his dick the woman just giggles. 'What's that?' says the man. The girl titters and says, 'Well I guess that's what my mummy would call a **'pee-pee'**. I don't know though, I haven't seen one before.' This is good enough for the man, so he asks her to marry him. On their wedding night, his bride asks to see his pee-pee again. 'Look,' says the man. 'Since we're married now, you can stop calling it a pee-pee. Call it a "dick".' 'Oh, you big silly,' giggles the bride. **'That's not a dick. A dick is ten inches long, three inches wide and black.'**

A man is in a pub playing the fruit machines when his wife rings him on his mobile and tells him to come home. 'I can't leave now,' says the man. 'I'm on a winning streak. I've got a pile of £1 coins as tall as my dick.' **'What!?'** shouts his wife. **'You mean you're down to three quid?'**

Men are like miniskirts:
watch out or they'll creep up your legs.

Men are like public toilets:
the good ones are engaged and the rest are full of crap.

Men are like trains:
they always stop before you get off.

Men are like bananas:
the older they are, the softer they get.

A man marries a girl from a very sheltered background. On their first night together he shows her his dick and, thinking it might stop her playing around in the future, tells her it's the only one in the world. A week later his bride says, 'You remember that thing you showed me? You said you had the only one in the world.' 'That's right,' replies the man. 'Well, it's not true,' says the bride. 'The man next door has one as well.' The man thinks quickly and replies, 'Well, yes, I used to have two, but that man is such a good friend, I gave him one of mine.' His wife whines, 'Awww, but why did you have to give him the *best* one?'

A married couple are broke and the only way they can make some money is if the wife **goes on the game**. The wife puts an ad in the paper and gets her first client. She takes the man into her bedroom and he asks how much she charges for sex. The wife doesn't know, so she goes downstairs and asks her husband. **'Tell him it's £70,'** he says. Back upstairs the wife tells the man the price, but he tells her he only has £20. The wife goes downstairs and asks her husband what £20 can buy.

'Tell him £20 is the price of a blowjob,' says the husband. The wife goes upstairs, tells her customer what he'll get for £20, and the man starts to strip off. The man drops his pants and the wife's eyes pop-out at the **huge size** of his dick. She runs downstairs and says to her husband,

'Here, can you lend me £50?'

Mrs Cohen, Mrs Levy, and Mrs Levine are talking about their sons. Mrs Cohen says, 'My Benjamin is a very successful lawyer. He has a penthouse apartment in LA, and a summer home in the south of France.' Mrs Levy says, 'Well let me tell you about my Samuel. He's a famous doctor who was nominated for a Nobel Prize.' Mrs Levine says, 'Well, my Isaac might not be rich or famous, but his dick is so long, ten pigeons can perch on it in a line.' Mrs Cohen says, 'Actually, I should confess. I was exaggerating. My Benjamin's an up-and-coming lawyer, but he doesn't have a penthouse or a summer home.' Mrs Levy says, 'I've got a confession too. Samuel is a wonderful doctor but he's never won a Nobel Prize.' Mrs Cohen and Mrs Levy look at Mrs Levine. 'Well, okay,' says Mrs Levine. 'So the last

pigeon has to stand
on one leg!'

Men are like chocolate: **they're
sweet, smooth, and usually
head right for your hips.**

Men are like photocopiers:
**you only need them for
reproduction.**

Men are like second-hand cars:
**they're cheap, easy to find
and unreliable.**

A guy snuggles up to his girlfriend and says, 'Hey, why don't we try a different position tonight?' 'What a great idea,' says the girlfriend. **'I know – you stand by the sink while I sit on the couch and fart.'**

A woman hears a knock on her front door. She opens it and finds a young homeless guy begging for spare change. She's about to shut the door when she notices the guy's **huge shoes**. She remembers the story that men with big feet have **equally big penises**, so she invites the man in. Next morning the homeless guy wakes after a night of sex and finds £50 and a note pinned to his pillow. The note reads, **'Buy some shoes that fit!'**

The King of Spain, the King of France, and the King of England are standing on a stage. They're having a competition to see who has the biggest dick. The King of Spain drops his pants. The people see his big dick and shout, **'Viva Espania!'** The King of France drops his pants. The people see his huge dick and shout, **'Vive la France!'** Last, the King of England drops his pants. There's a stunned silence, then the people cry, **'God save the Queen!'**

Two old ladies go to the zoo where they see an angry male elephant running about with a **huge erection**. 'Oh dear,' says one old lady. **'D'you think he'll charge?'** The other old lady looks at the elephant's crotch and says, **'Well, yes. I think he'd be entitled to.'**

Two guys are on a beach. One of them is getting a lot of attention from the girls, and the other guy can't understand why. The first guy reveals his secret. 'It's easy,' he says. 'Just drop a potato down your swimming trunks and walk around for a bit. The girls will be queuing up.' The second guy takes this advice, stuffs a potato down his trunks, and parades up and down the beach. Things do not go well however, and the ladies are not impressed at all, in fact, they seem to want to keep as far away from him as possible. Baffled, the guy goes back to his friend who immediately sees the problem, 'You're meant to put the potato down the *front* of your trunks…'

What's pink and drags along the bottom of the sea?
Moby's Dick.

What's white and 12 inches long?
Absolutely nothing!

A woman in a card shop spends 20 minutes browsing the shelves, but she can't find what she wants. Eventually she goes to the manager and says, 'Excuse me. Do you have any **'Sorry I laughed at your penis' cards?'**

A man is embarrassed about the size of his dick and worried that his latest girlfriend will think it's **too small**. Eventually he decides to reveal the problem. While they're kissing on the sofa, he undoes his zip and guides her hand inside his trousers. **'No thanks,'** says the girl. **'I don't smoke.'**

Eight More Things You Probably Shouldn't Say To A Naked Man

1 Ah, isn't it cute.

2 Why don't we just cuddle?

3 It's more fun to look at.

4 Tell you what, why don't we skip straight to the cigarettes?

5 At least this won't take long.

6 I hear too much wanking shrinks it.

7 But it still works, right?

8 I didn't know they came that small.

A mother and daughter are talking about the facts of life. The girl says, 'Mummy, what's a penis?' Mother replies, 'That's what your father pees with.' The girl says, 'So what's a prick?' **Her mother says,** 'That's the bit that's attached to the penis.'

BLONDES
HAVE MORE FUN

A handsome Italian picks up a blonde in a Naples nightclub. He talks her into bed and they spend 20 minutes having energetic sex. When he's done, the Italian lights a cigarette. 'You finish?' he asks in broken English. 'No,' replies the blonde. The Italian wants his new lady friend to be satisfied so he starts again. After 40 minutes, the girl seems to have had enough. 'You finish?' says the Italian. 'No,' replies the blonde. The astonished Italian has another go. He gives it all he's got and uses every trick in the book. After 50 minutes, he collapses beside the blonde. 'Are you finish?' he gasps. 'No,' replies the blonde. The Italian can't believe it, but his reputation is at stake, so he launches into one final effort. Finally, after an hour of high-octane sex, the shattered Italian croaks, 'You, you finish now?' 'No,' replies the blonde. 'What?' says the Italian. 'How can you not be finish?' The blonde replies, 'Because I'm Swedish.'

A blonde goes to see her doctor after an operation. 'Doc,' she says. 'How long do I have to wait before I can start having sex?' 'You could have it now if you wanted,' replies the doctor. 'Y'know, that's the first time anyone's asked me that after having their tonsils out.'

Have you heard about 'blonde paint'? **It's not very bright, but it's cheap and spreads easy.**

How does a blonde hold her liquor? **By the ears.**

What did the blonde's mother say to her before she went out on a date?

'If you're not in bed by midnight, come home.'

What do blondes put behind their ears to attract men?
Their knees.

Two blondes are visiting a zoo when they come across a **gorilla sticking its huge erection** through the bars of its cage. One of the blondes reaches out to have a feel, but the gorilla grabs her and drags her into its enclosure. The gorilla then has **sex with the blonde** for an hour while the zoo staff run around trying to find a vet to tranquilise him. Eventually, someone shoots a dart into the sex-crazed gorilla and it collapses. The blonde is rescued and rushed to hospital. A couple of days later the blonde's friend drops by to see how she is. 'Are you hurt?' asks the friend. **'Am I hurt?'** sobs the blonde. **'It's been two days and he hasn't called, he hasn't written...'**

What's the difference between a blonde and a Jumbo jet?

Not everyone's been in a Jumbo jet.

What does a blonde do first thing in the morning?

She introduces herself and walks home.

What's the mating call of the blonde?

'I'm so drunk.'

What's the mating call of the ugly blonde?

'I said, 'I'm sooo drunk!!!''

Brunette: **'My boyfriend bought me flowers for Valentine's Day, I guess that means he'll want my legs in the air.'**
Blonde: **'Why? Don't you have a vase?'**

GREAT BIG
LONG ONES

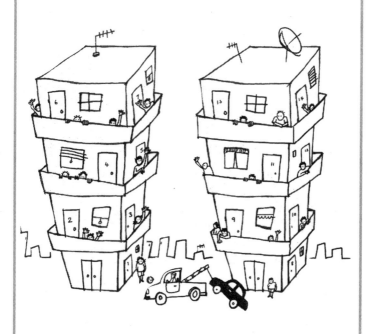

Teacher asks her class for a sentence with the word 'contagious' **in it. Little Suzie sticks her hand up, 'Miss. My dad and me were driving along, when we saw a fruit truck that had** spilt melons **all over the road. The driver was trying to put them back in the truck, and dad said it would take that** contagious **to pick them all up.'**

An old lady goes to see a doctor about a **problem with her sex drive**. 'I don't seem to have as much fun in bed as I used to,' she says. 'I see,' says the doctor. 'And how old are you and your husband.' **'I'm 82,'** says the old lady. **'And my husband is 77.'** 'And when did you first notice the problem?' asks the doctor. The old lady replies, **'Twice last night and once again this morning.'**

A man walks into a store and asks for a tub of vanilla ice-cream, a tub of strawberry ice-cream, and a tub of chocolate ice-cream. 'Sorry,' says the woman at the counter. 'We're out of chocolate ice-cream.' 'Okay,' says the man, 'I'll have a tub of tutti-frutti, a tub of coffee and a tub of chocolate.' 'Are you deaf?' says the woman. 'I just told you, we don't have any chocolate ice-cream.' 'Okay,' says the man. 'Then I'll have a tub of toffee, a tub of rum-and-raisin, and a tub of chocolate.' 'Listen,' says the woman. 'What does the V-A-N in vanilla spell?' 'Van,' says the man. 'That's right,' says the woman. 'And what does the S-T-R-A-W in strawberry spell?' 'Straw,' says the man. 'Fine,' says the woman. 'So what does the F-U-C-K in chocolate spell?' The man says, 'There's no fuck in chocolate?' 'That's right!' says the woman. 'And that's what I've been trying to tell you!'

A dumb-looking blonde walks into a doctor's office. The doctor is a randy pervert. He tells her to strip off then starts **stroking her legs**. 'Do you know what I'm doing?' asks the doctor. 'Um? Checking for varicose veins?' replies the blonde. Then the doctor starts **rubbing her boobs**. 'D'you know what I'm doing now?' he says. 'Duh? Looking for lumps?' replies the blonde. Then the doctor tells her to lie on the examining table and **climbs on top of her**. 'Do you know what I'm doing now?' asks the doctor. 'Yeah,' snaps the blonde. **'Getting crabs – that's what I'm here for!'**

An old geezer totters through the door of a brothel. The doorman stops him. 'What are you looking for, granddad?' he says. 'You sure you're in the right place?' 'Is this where all the hot women are?' says the old man. 'Because I'm after a good time.' 'How old are you, pop?' asks the doorman. 'I'm 92,' replies the old man. '92!' says the doorman 'Boy, you've had it, gramps'. The old man looks confused 'I have?' he says, taking out his wallet. 'How much do I owe you?'

A farmer and his son go to market to buy a cow. The farmer finds a cow he likes and prods it all over: he strokes its belly, rubs its back and legs, and even peers up its rear end. 'You see, son,' explains the farmer. 'If you're going to pay for something, you have to **give it a real good going over to see if it's worth the money**.' Next day, the boy runs up to his father and says, **'Dad! Dad! I just saw mummy and the uncle Jack behind the barn. I think he's planning on buying her!'**

A girl throws a fancy dress party where everyone has to come as a human emotion. **The first guest arrives covered in green paint with the letters** N **and** V **painted on his chest. 'So what are you?' asks the hostess.** 'I'm green with en-vy,' **says the guest. The next to arrive is a woman in a** pink bodystocking with a feather boa **wrapped around her boobs and fanny. 'And what emotion are you?' asks the hostess. The woman says,** 'I'm tickled pink.' **Next up are two of the hostess' Jamaican friends, Wardell and Delroy. Wardell is** naked and has his dick stuck in a bowl of custard. **Delroy is also naked, but his** dick is stuck in a pear. **'I give up,' says the hostess. 'What emotions are you?' 'It's easy,' replies Wardell.** 'I'm fucking disgusted, and Delroy has come in despair.'

Teacher reminds her class about an **important exam** that's taking place the next day. 'I won't tolerate any excuses for non-attendance tomorrow,' she says. Billy, the **class clown** sticks up his hand. 'Miss,' he says. 'What would you say if I rang in tomorrow and said I was **suffering from sexual exhaustion?**' Teacher replies, 'In that case, Billy. I'd tell you to come into school and **do the test with your other hand**.'

A couple and their son live in an apartment in the city. One Sunday the couple decide to have an afternoon quickie and ask the son to stand out on the balcony and tell them what's going on in the neighbourhood. They figure this will give them some privacy and keep her occupied for a few minutes. The couple go to their bedroom and the son begins his commentary.

'There's a car being clamped by the school,' he says. 'An ambulance and a police car just drove by. They're having a sale at the sofa store. An old lady is feeding the birds.' A few moments later she calls out. 'I just saw the vicar. And Mr and Mrs Carter are having sex.' Mum and dad rush out of the bedroom.

'What?' cries mum. 'How do you know the Carters are having sex?' The son replies, 'Because their son is standing out on the balcony too.'

78-year-old Hilda announces that she's going to marry her 19-year-old window cleaner. Hilda's doctor hears about this and goes to visit her. 'I think you ought to reconsider this marriage,' he says. 'It could be very dangerous. Prolonged sex with a young man could be fatal.' Hilda shrugs and says, 'If he dies, he dies.'

A man finds a magic lamp. He rubs it and releases a genie. 'What is your wish?' asks the genie. 'I love sex,' **says the man.** 'So I want to be hard all the time, and get more ass than any man who ever lived.' **So the genie** turns him into a toilet bowl.

A woman complains to her boss that a co-worker is sexually harassing **her. 'So what does this guy do?' asks the boss. The woman replies, 'Every morning he stands right up next to me and tells me** my hair smells nice!' **'Well, that sounds okay,' says the boss. 'Why don't you take it as a compliment.' 'I would,' replies the woman.** 'Except the little creep is a midget!'

Teacher says to her class, 'Who can tell me the meaning of indifferent?' **Little Suzie puts up her hand.** 'It means 'lovely', miss.' **'No. That's not right,' says teacher. Suzie replies,** 'Yes it is, miss. Last night I heard mummy say, 'That's lovely', **and daddy said,** 'Yeah, it's in different.''

A **randy mouse** comes across a female elephant with a thorn in her foot. **'I can pull that thorn out,'** says the mouse. **'But I'll want a favour in return – I want to have sex with you.'** The elephant tries not to laugh. 'Well, okay,' she says. **'If you can get the thorn out, you can do what you like.'** So the mouse pulls out the thorn then climbs up on a tree-stump to collect his reward. The elephant backs into position. 'Let me know when you've finished,' says the elephant. The mouse prepares to get started. At that moment, an eagle flying overhead **loses its grip on a tortoise it's been carrying**. The tortoise plummets down and **hits the elephant on the head**. **'Ouch!'** says the elephant. **'Oh yeah,'** says the mouse. **'Yeah. You like that, don't you, baby...'**

Two women are **playing golf**. One of them tees off, but the ball slices sideways and **hits a man standing nearby**. The man **clasps his hands together over his crotch and falls to the ground in agony.** The woman rushes over. 'I'm sorry,' she says. 'Please let me help. I'm a physical therapist. **I know just what to do**.' So the woman pulls down the man's trousers and pants and **starts giving the man's privates an expert massage**. After a few moments the man seems to have calmed down. 'How does that feel?' asks the woman. **'That feels great,'** says the man. **'But I think you broke my thumb.'**

To save money Susan and Tony have their honeymoon at a boarding house run by Susan's mother. Susan's never seen a man naked before and she's very nervous. Tony takes his shirt off and reveals his broad hairy chest. Susan runs downstairs and says, 'Mum! Tony has hair all over his chest. I that normal?' 'Of course it is,' replies mother. 'I like a man with a hairy chest.' Susan goes back upstairs and sees Tony taking off his trousers. She runs downstairs and says, 'Mum! Tony has a tiny tight bum. Is that normal?' 'Yes,' replies mother. 'I like a man with a small bum.' Susan goes upstairs and finds Tony completely naked. She rushes downstairs again. 'Mum! Mum! I just saw Tony's thingy – it's over a foot long! Is that normal?' Mum shakes her head. 'No it isn't, dear,' she says. 'That's not normal at all. You stay down here – this sounds like a job for mummy.'

Teacher says, 'Children, if **you could have one element** in the world, what would it be?' Little Jimmy says, **'I'd want gold. Then I could buy a Porsche.'** Little Billy says, **'I'd want platinum. Platinum is worth more than gold.** I could buy a Porsche and a Ferrari.' Little Suzie says, **'I want some silicone.'** 'Silicone?' says teacher. 'That's not very valuable.' 'That's what you think,' says Little Suzie. **'My mummy's got two bags of the stuff and you should see all the sports cars outside *our* house!'**

SHARP
TONGUE
ACTION

Can I buy you a drink? What are you having?

This minute? An attack of nausea!

I know a fantastic way to burn off some calories.

Me too. It involves running the hell away from you.

So tell me, how did a creep like you beat 1,000,000 other sperm?

Some men are arrogant and rude. But you're completely the opposite – you're rude and arrogant!

If ignorance is bliss, you must be in the middle of one long orgasm.

Do you kiss with your eyes closed?
With you I would.

A hard-on doesn't count as personal growth.

**I'd go to the
ends of the earth
for you.**

I'm sure you would
– but would you
stay there?'

Come on, don't be shy. Ask me out.
Sure. Get out!

Let's be honest, we both came to this bar for the same reason.
Really? You're here to pick up chicks too?

Why don't you come back to my flat for some heavy breathing?
Why, is your lift out of order?

Try all you like, but you'll never be the man your mother was!

So how do you like your eggs in the morning?
Unfertilised!

I like the way you dye the roots of your hair brown.
Yeah? Well at least I've *got* some roots.

I bet I know what you use for contraception – your personality.

I thought I saw your name on a loaf of bread this morning. But when I looked again it actually said, 'Thick cut'.

Baby, I'd go through anything for you.
Fantastic! Let's start with your savings account!

Do you know the best way to practice safe sex? Go screw yourself!

I'd like to see things from your point of view, but I could never get my head so far up my backside.

If I'd known I was going to run into a girl as beautiful as you, I'd have plucked my nostrils.

And if I'd known I was going to meet someone looking like you, I'd have plucked my eyeballs.

If you kiss me, I promise I won't turn into a frog.

So why would I want to kiss you?

It was fantastic meeting you tonight. Why don't we do it again?

Because I'd rather die.

I've got a couple of cinema tickets. Want to go?

Sure, but only if I get both of them.

My ideal woman has to have a great sense of humour.

Looking at you – she'd need one!

So what does a sweet thing like you do for a living?

I'm a female impersonator.

If I asked you to marry me, what would you say?

Nothing. I get the hiccups when I try to talk and laugh at the same time.

What's it like being the best-looking person in the room?

You'll never know.

Put a sock in it! A man with your IQ should have a low voice too!

Your figure is turning a few heads.

And your face is turning a few stomachs.

Are you trying to imagine me naked?

No. I'm trying to imagine you with a personality.

Are these your eyeballs? I just found them in my cleavage.

Every man has the right to be ugly, but don't abuse the privilege!

You're as much use as a condom vending machine in the Vatican!

When shall we meet up again?
How about never? Is never good for you?

I'd love to go out with you tonight, but I'm really busy – my favourite baked bean commercial might be on the telly this evening.

Do you know what – we'd all be a lot happier if your dad had settled for a **blowjob.**

EACH
TO THEIR
OWN DEVICES

I'm better at sex than anyone I know. Now all I need is a partner.

A woman goes to her doctor for a check up. The doctor examines her and finds a large lump of pink wax in her navel. 'How did that get there?' he asks. 'Well, it's sort of embarrassing,' says the woman. 'But my boyfriend likes to eat by candle-light...'

Tracy decides to surprise her boyfriend and buys a pair of **crotchless knickers**. She's lying on the bed when her boyfriend comes in. Tracy spreads her legs and says, 'Hey, big boy. Fancy some of this?' **'Christ no!'** shrieks her boyfriend. **'Look what it's done to your pants!'**

A guy walks into a bar looking miserable. 'What's up?' asks the barman. 'I've just discovered my oldest son is gay,' **replies the man. A week later, the man comes back looking even more depressed. He says to the barman,** 'I've just discovered my second son is gay as well.' **A week later he's back again, looking suicidal.** 'This morning my youngest son told me he's gay too,' **says the man. 'Jeez,' says the barman.** 'So does anyone in your family like women?' 'Yeah,' **sighs the man.** 'It turns out my wife does.'

If you mix Viagra and Prozac you end up with a guy who's ready to go, but doesn't really care where.

A little old man totters into a chemist's to buy Viagra. 'Can I have six tablets, please,' he says. 'And I need them cut into quarters.' 'I could cut them up,' says the chemist. 'But a quarter of a tablet won't give you a full erection.' 'I'm 96,' says the old man. 'I don't have much use for an erection. I just want it sticking out far enough so I don't piss over my slippers.'

An old lady staggers into a sex shop. She hobbles to the counter and grabs it for support. 'D-d-do y-y-yo-o-u s-s-s-ell v-v-v-vibr-br-rators?' she says. 'Sure,' replies the sales clerk. 'We've got lots of them.' The old lady gasps, 'D-d-d-do y-y-you ha-have a-a-a-a b-b-big r-r-red o-o-one, e-e-e-ight i-i-i-inches l-l-long c-c-c-alled Th-th-the P-p-p-punish-sh-sher?' The clerk replies, 'Yeah, we do sell that one.' 'I-i-in th-th-that c-ca-case,' says the little old lady, 'C-c-could y-y-ou t-t-tell m-m-m h-how t-to t-t-tturn th-th-the fu-fu-fucking th-th-th-thing o-o-off?'

A father finds his son in the shed banging a nail into the wall. 'That's a big nail,' says father. 'It's not a nail,' **says the boy.** 'It's a worm. I mixed some stuff from my chemistry set, dipped this worm in it and it became as hard as steel.' **Father is impressed. 'Tell you what,' he says. 'Give me your formula and I'll buy you a car.' The boy agrees and the next day he and his dad go and look in the garage. Parked inside are a second-hand Volkswagen and a brand new Ferrari. 'Wow,' says the boy. 'Which one's mine.' 'Both,' replies father.** 'I got you the Volkswagen. The Ferrari's from your mother.'

A woman goes to the doctor's with a vibrator jammed up her pussy. 'Get on the examination table,' says the doctor. 'I'll have it out in a minute.' 'Get it out?' says the woman. 'I don't want it out. I want you to change the batteries!'

Two couples decide to spice up their sex live by swapping partners. Later that night, one of the guys rolls over in bed and says, 'Hey. I wonder what our wives are up to?'

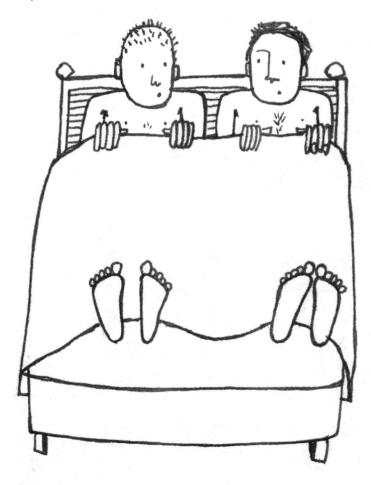

A woman goes to her doctor with a problem – her husband isn't interested in sex any more and she wants the doctor to give her some pep-pills The doctor gives her a small bottle of tablets. 'These are new,' he says. 'They're very powerful and they may have side-effects we don't know about. Whatever happens, your husband must not take more than one a month!' The woman goes home, but she's too embarrassed to ask her husband to take a pep pill so she decides to slip him a tablet in a cup of coffee. She makes him a cup, but drops in two tablets by mistake. The woman doesn't want to waste the tablets so she stirs them in, drinks half the coffee herself and gives the rest to her husband in the next room. She thinks it might take an hour or two for the tablet to work, but seconds later, her husband storms into the room looking wild-eyed. He tears off his sweat-soaked shirt and shouts 'I want a woman! I want a woman right now!!' The woman gulps and wipes a bead of sweat from her forehead 'You know what?' she gulps. 'I think I want one too.'

Sandra comes home early from work. She goes into the living room, and **finds her naked husband kneeling on the carpet having sex with the vicar's wife doggy-style.** 'You bastard!' she yells. 'I knew you were seeing other women, but **this time you've gone too far!' 'You're right,'** moans hubby. **'I think I'm stuck.'**

Suzanne is telling her friend Jane about **a sex game** she plays with her boyfriend. 'We get naked and sit opposite each other on the floor,' she says. 'Then **my boyfriend throws grapes at my pussy and I throw doughnuts over his dick**. If he gets a grape in my pussy, he eats it; and if I get a doughnut over his erection, I get to eat that.' 'I'm going to try that with my boyfriend,' says Jane. 'D'you think the corner shop will still be open?' 'It might be,' says Suzanne. 'But I don't think they sell doughnuts or grapes.' **'I don't need doughnuts or grapes,'** says Jane. **'I need a box of Cheerio's and a sack of apples.'**

My boyfriend wanted to be an unstoppable sex machine, but he failed the practical.

INTIMATE
PROBLEMS

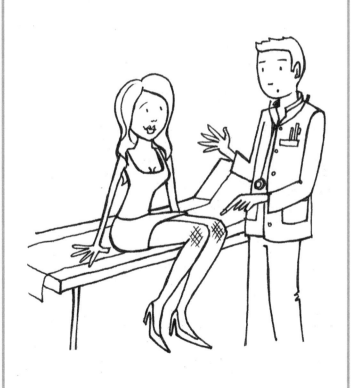

Women's Problems

MEN strual cramps
MEN opause
GUY naecologist
And if things get really bad,
a...**HIS** terectomy.

Can it really be a coincidence that all women's problems start with men?!

A doctor tells a woman patient that her pussy is almost burnt out from too much sex – she can only use it another 30 times before it packs in. The woman goes home and tells her husband the news. 'That's terrible,' he says. 'With so few left we can't waste any – let's make a list of special occasions.' 'Sorry,' says the woman. 'I already made a list – you're not on it.'

A man suffering from premature ejaculation goes to see his doctor. As a cure, the doctor suggests that the man tries to **startle himself** when he's about to come – something that makes a loud noise should do it. The man goes home, but returns the next day with a **bandage round his dick**.

'What happened?' asks the doctor.

'Well, doc,' says the man. 'I bought a starter pistol to make a loud noise. Then I ran home and found my wife naked in the bedroom. We got straight to it and **started having some 69.** I felt myself coming so **I fired the gun. Then my wife crapped on my head, bit two inches off my dick, and my neighbour jumped out of the wardrobe with his hands in the air.'**

A man discovers that **his dick has gone green** and goes to a doctor. 'I'm sorry,' says the doctor. 'I can't cure it. We're going to have to **amputate**.' The man is horrified and goes to get a second opinion. 'I'm sorry,' says the second doctor. 'But your dick has **got to come off**.' The man won't accept this, so he seeks a third opinion. 'I've got good news and bad news,' says the third doctor. 'The good news is that we **don't have to cut your dick off**.' 'What a relief,' says the man, 'So what's the bad news?' The doctor replies, **'It just fell on the floor.'**

A woman with sore knees goes to see her doctor. 'It might be my sex life,' says the woman. 'My boyfriend and I make love four times a week and we always do it 'doggy style'.' 'There are other positions,' says the doctor. 'Yes,' says the woman.
'But not if you want to watch Coronation Street as well.'

A woman with a mild hormone imbalance is put on a course of testosterone tablets. A week later she comes back to her doctor for a check-up. 'Since I've been taking the pills, I've noticed some extra hair growth,' says the woman. 'That's not unusual,' says the doctor. 'Where are you growing this hair?' The woman replies,

'On my balls.'

A man is lying in a hospital bed with an oxygen mask over his face. A nurse arrives to sponge him down. 'Nurse,' mumbles the man, 'are my testicles black?' **'I don't know,' replies the nurse. 'I'm only here to wash you.' The man says,** 'But, nurse, are my testicles black?' **'I really don't know,' says the nurse. Again, the man asks,** 'Nurse, can you tell me if my testicles are black?' **The nurse gives in. She lifts up the man's gown, picks up his dick and takes a good look at his balls.** 'No,' **she says.** 'They're pink.' **The man pulls off his oxygen mask and says,** 'Thanks, but are my test results back!?'

Two men get talking in a doctor's waiting room. 'Why are you here?' asks one. 'I have a **red ring around my dick**,' replies the other. 'How about you?' The first man says, 'I've got a **green ring round my dick**.' The doctor then calls in the man with the red ring. After a few minutes the man walks out with a relieved look on his face – the doctor's told him he's going to be fine. Then it's the turn of the man with the green ring. The man goes into the doctor's office and drops his trousers. 'Bad news,' says the doctor. 'Your penis is about to drop off.' 'What?!' says the man. 'You told the guy with the red ring that he was going to be okay!' 'Yes,' replies the doctor. **'But there's a big difference between lipstick and gangrene.'**

They now have a thing called 'Marriage Anonymous'. If you ever feel like getting married, you call them up and they send round an unshaven man in a dirty tee-shirt who'll sit in front of your TV for three days farting, drinking beer and asking for the occasional blowjob.

GIRLS
ON TOP

In the early hours of the morning, **a cop sees a car weaving over the road.** He pulls it over and finds a young woman at the wheel, **stinking of booze.** The cop asks her to **blow in a Breathalyzer** and looks at the indicator strip. 'I thought so,' he says. 'It **looks like you've had four or five stiff ones tonight.'** 'You're kidding?' says the woman. 'You mean it can tell that too?'

A man and a woman have an argument about **who enjoys sex more; men or women**. The man says, 'Men must enjoy sex more – we spend all our time trying to get laid.' 'That doesn't prove anything,' says the woman. **'When your ear itches and you wiggle your finger in it, which feels better – your ear or your finger?'**

A market researcher stops three women in the street and asks them **how they know if they've had a good night out**. The first woman says, 'If I come home, get undressed, climb into bed and **lay there tingling all over**, I know I've had a good night out.' The second one says, 'If I come home, get undressed, climb into bed and feel like **I'm riding a roller-coaster**, I know I've had a good night out.' The third says, **'I come home, get undressed, and throw my knickers at the wall; if they stick I know I've had a *damn* good night out!'**

A man is downing a glass of champagne in a bar when he sees a woman doing the same. 'Are you celebrating?' he asks. 'Yes,' replies the woman. 'I thought I was infertile, but my doctor's just told me I'm pregnant.' 'Congratulations,' says the man. 'I'm celebrating too. I'm a chicken farmer and my hens haven't been laying for months. But I eventually figured out what was wrong – I changed cocks.' 'That's a coincidence,' says the woman. 'Me too!'

A woman runs into her house and finds her husband in the living room, **'Pack your bags!'** she says. **'I just won the lottery!'** 'Fantastic!' says the husband. **'What should I pack? Where are we going?'** 'Go where you like,' replies the woman, **'just hurry up and fuck off!'**

Two friends go for a **girls-night-out** on the town. They get really drunk and on the way home they **duck into a cemetery for a pee**. Once they've finished, one woman wipes herself dry on her **knickers** and **throws them away**, while the other woman wipes herself with a **piece of paper she find pinned to a wreath**. The following morning their boyfriends are comparing notes. One says, **'I think we need to start keeping a closer eye on those two. Mine came home last night without any underwear!'** The other says, **'You think that's bad. When my girlfriend came home she had a card stuck to her pussy saying, 'We will never forget you."**

An elderly couple get married. **On their honeymoon, the husband takes off his glasses and goes to clean his teeth, while his bride does some yoga. She gets naked and does a stretching exercise on the bed, lying on her back and lifting her legs up and over her head.** Unfortunately her feet get stuck in the headboard. **She calls for help and her husband dashes in. He peers at her and says,** 'For Christ's sake, Mavis. Brush your hair and put your teeth in. You look just like your mother!'

Two girlfriends are talking. One says, 'That bloke I picked up last night turned out to be a right bastard. **After we'd had sex, he called me a slag!**' 'Never!' says her friend. 'What did you do?' The first girl replies, **'I told him to get out of my bed and take his bleedin' mates with him.'**

Three hillbilly gals are sitting in a bar, chewing the fat. One says, **'If ma husband were a soda pop, I'd call him '7-Up'. Because he's got seven inches and it's always up!'** The second gal says, **'Well if mine was a soda pop, I'd call him 'Mountain Dew' because he can 'mount' and 'dew' me anytime!'** The third says, **'Well I'd call mine 'Southern Comfort'.'** **'Southern Comfort?'** says the first gal. **'That's no soda pop, that's a hard liquor.'** The third woman replies, **'Yup, that's him alright!'**

A man goes into a magic shop and sees a pair of 'nudie' glasses for sale. 'What do they do?' asks the man. 'They let you see everyone in the nude,' says the storekeeper. 'Why not try them on.' So the man tries on the glasses and straightaway everyone he looks at is in the nude. The storekeeper is nude, his assistant is nude, even a passer-by looking in the window is nude. The man buys the glasses and goes out into the street to look at everyone in the nude. After an hour of fun he decides to sneak home and surprise his wife with his new toy. He gets back, creeps in the living room, and finds his wife and his neighbour nude on the couch. 'Surprise!' he shouts, coming into the room. 'What do you think of my new glasses?' He takes them off and is surprised to see that his wife and neighbour are still naked. 'Damn!' he says. 'I've only had them an hour and they're broken already!'

Woman, to man: 'You want sex?'

Man: 'Your place or mine?'

Woman: 'Well if you're going to argue – forget it!'

Why do men find it hard to make eye contact?

Because breasts don't have eyes.

Two midgets pick up a couple of girls and take them back to their hotel. The first midget is unable to get a hard-on, and hearing his friend in the next room doesn't make him feel any better – all night long, all he hears through the wall is his friend shouting, 'One, two, three... Uuuhh!! One, two, three... Uuuhh!!' The next morning, the midgets compare notes. The first midget says, 'It was really embarrassing. I tried everything but I couldn't get an erection.' 'You think *that's* embarrassing?' says the second midget. 'I couldn't even get up on the bed!'

A woman sees a plastic surgeon about the bags under her eyes. **The surgeon removes the bags then** puts a small crank in the back of the woman's head. **He tells her to turn the crank if she notices any new bags forming – this will** tighten up the skin **and the bags will disappear. This technique** works for many years, **but one day an enormous pair of bags appear under the woman's eyes, and no amount of cranking will get rid of them. The surgeon examines her and says,** 'No wonder you can't get rid of those bags – they're your breasts. You've been turning that crank much too hard.' 'Oh dear,' **says the woman.** 'And I suppose that would also explain the goatee.'

What does a 75-year-old woman have between her boobs that a 25-year-old doesn't? **Her navel.**

A guy hooks up with a girl in a bar and they end up **back at her place**. After a night of non-stop bonking the guy gets up and takes a shower. As he's drying off, he sees **a photo of a man on the girl's dressing table**. The man **looks like a nasty piece of work, a real hard-nut**, and the **guy starts to worry**. **'Who's that a picture of?'** asks the guy. **'It's not your**

husband, or a boyfriend, is it?' '**Nah,**' replies the girl. **'That's me before the operation.'**

LET'S GET
IT ON

A woman goes to a doctor and tells him that her husband is 300% impotent. '300% impotent!,' **says the doc. 'I'm not sure I understand what you mean.' The woman says,** 'He can't get an erection; last week he broke his fingers; and this morning he burned his tongue!'

A divorce lawyer is speaking to his client, Sandra. 'Your husband says you lied to him,' says the lawyer. **'That's crap,'** says Sandra. **'He lied to me. He said he'd be out till midnight, and the bastard came home at 9.30.'**

Why are married women heavier than single women? Single women come home, see what's in the fridge and go to bed. Married women come home, see what's in bed and go to the fridge.

A couple are saving up for their holiday and the husband has the idea of putting some money in a cash box every time they have sex. **A month later he counts the money and finds over £800. 'Where did all that come from?' asks the husband.** 'I was only putting in £20 a go.' **'You might have been,' replies his wife.** 'But not everyone's as stingy as you are!'

A man comes home early from work and finds his wife **having sex** with a midget from the local circus. **'What?!'** he cries. **'First it was the world's tallest man, then it was a trapeze artist, then the lion tamer, and now it's a midget!'** 'Oh **come on,'** says his wife. **'At least I'm cutting back.'**

A couple are having sex. The woman says, **'You haven't got AIDS have you?'** 'No,' replies the man. 'Thank fuck for that!' says the woman. **'I wouldn't like to catch *that* again!'**

What a woman says:

Come on. This place is a mess! You and I need to clean. Your pants are on the floor and you'll have no clothes if we don't do the laundry now!

What a man hears:

Come on...Blah, blah, blah...YOU AND I...blah, blah, blah, blah, blah...ON THE FLOOR...blah, blah, blah...NO CLOTHES... blah, blah, blah, blah...NOW!

Lorenzo, the Italian stallion, walks into a bar looking worried. 'Hey, Lorenzo,' says the barman. 'Why the long face?' 'Some pissed-off husband sent me a letter,' says Lorenzo. 'He said he'd cut my balls off and make me eat them if I didn't stop screwing his wife.' 'So why don't you stop?' asks the barman. 'I can't,' says Lorenzo. 'He didn't sign his name!'

How do you know if elephants have been having sex in your kitchen? The bin-liners are missing.

A husband thinks his wife is having an affair, so he bursts into their high-rise apartment **to catch her in the act**. He finds his wife naked on the bed, but **can't see a man anywhere**. He looks around the flat, then glances out of the window and **sees a man running down the stairs**. The husband looks around for a missile then **picks up the kitchen fridge and lobs it out of the window**. The fridge lands on the man as he's running across the car park and flattens him. The husband has had his revenge, but the strain of lifting the fridge was too much and he **drops dead from a heart attack**. A few minutes later, the husband is queuing outside the Pearly Gates with two other men. One of the men asks him how he died. **'I picked up something heavy and had a heart attack,'** says the husband. 'You won't believe what happened to me,' says the man. **'I was running for a bus when some bastard dropped a heavy weight on me.' 'That's nothing,'** says the third man. **'I was hiding in this fridge...'**

Psychiatrist, to woman: 'When you make love, do you ever look your husband in the eyes.'

Woman: 'Yes, but I only did it once – he looked very, very angry.''

Psychiatrist: 'And why do you think that was?'

Woman: 'Because he was looking-in through the bedroom window.'

You should always talk to your boyfriend when you're having sex – **assuming** there's a phone handy.

A woman sneaks up behind her husband and hits him over the head with her shoe. 'What the hell was that for!?' shouts the man. 'You're having an affair!' says the woman. 'There was a piece of paper in your jacket pocket with 'Dirty Sally' written on it and a phone number.' 'That's the name of a horse!' exclaims the man. 'I called a bookie to make a bet.' Next day the woman sneaks up again. This time she hits her husband with a golf club. 'What is it now!?' cries the man. The woman replies, 'Your horse phoned!!'

Why did the Irishman wear two condoms?
To be sure, to be sure.

A girl goes up to her boyfriend and says, 'Do you want to hear something that will make you happy and sad at exactly the same time?' 'Go on,' says the boyfriend. 'Okay,' says the girl. 'Your dick is much, much bigger than your brother's.'

Boyfriend, to girl: 'Why can't I tell when you have an orgasm?'
Girl: 'Because you're never at home when it happens.'

A doctor and his wife have a row about their sex life. It ends with the doctor telling his wife that she's lousy in bed. The doctor goes to work where he calms down and realises he ought to apologise. He rings home **and waits, and waits, and waits for the phone to be picked up**. Eventually his wife answers. **'What took you so long?'** asks the doctor. 'Well,' says his wife. **'Y'know how you said I was lousy in bed.'** 'Yes,' says the doctor. The wife replies, **'Well I was getting a second opinion!'**

Posh boyfriend, to girl: 'You know, from the first time I ever saw you, I've wanted to make love to you terribly.'
Girl: 'Well, you've certainly done that...'

Man: 'Doctor, I suffer from premature ejaculation. Can you help me?!'
Doctor: 'No, but I can introduce you to a woman with a short attention span!'

A guy says to his friend, 'My girlfriend always laughs during sex. **It doesn't matter what she's reading.**'

A man and a woman get together in a bar. At the end of the night the pair end up having sex in the back of the man's car. The woman is insatiable – she wants more and more. Eventually the man staggers out for a break and sees a man changing the tyre on his truck. The man goes over and says, **'I've got a really hot date in my car, but I need a rest. Will you go in there and have sex with her till I've recovered – it's so dark she won't know the difference.'** The second man agrees and climbs into the back of the car, which soon starts to rock rhythmically. A policeman walks by. He shines a torch in the back of the car and says, 'What's all this then?' The man replies, 'I'm having sex with my wife.' 'Couldn't you do that in home?' asks the policeman. 'I could,' replies the man. **'But until you shone that torch in her face I didn't realize it *was* my wife.'**

One morning, a man walks into the kitchen and **finds his wife cooking breakfast in her dressing gown.** She turns to him and says, **'Don't say a word. Screw me right now, here**

on the table!' She whips off her dressing gown, lies back on the kitchen table and her husband makes passionate love to her. When they've finished, the man says, **'That was fantastic. But what's the occasion? Is it your birthday?'** 'No,' says his wife. **'I'm boiling an egg and the timer is broken.'**

An impotent man goes to a witchdoctor for help. **The witchdoctor casts a spell, then tells the man to say** 'One, two, three' if he wants an erection. **The erection will then stay rock-hard until someone says** 'One, two, three, four', at which point the erection will shrivel away. **There's a catch however, the spell can only be used once a year. The man is delighted. He rushes home, jumps into bed with his wife, and shouts** 'One, two, three.' **Puzzled, his wife says,** 'Why did you say 'One, two, three' for?'

A young couple have sex for the first time. It's over in a flash. The boy says, **'If I'd known you were a virgin, I would have taken more time.'** His girlfriend says, **'If I'd had more time, I would have taken off my tights!'**

Why do so many men suffer from premature ejaculation?

Because they have to rush back to the pub to tell their mates what they've been up to.

Did you hear about the idiot who filled his condom with ice?

He wanted to keep the swelling down!

A couple have sex for the first time. After it's over, the girl tells the guy he was lousy in bed. 'What d'you mean 'lousy'?' he says. 'How can you have any sort of opinion after only 15 seconds?'

One day a woman discovers that her husband is impotent – in fact, all their married life he's been using a strap-on dildo. 'That's awful,' says his wife. 'How could you lie to me like that?' 'I'm sorry, honey,' replies her husband. 'But, on the other hand, I'd be quite interested to hear you explain our three children.'

Last night my boyfriend made love to me for an hour and five minutes – it was the night they put the clocks forward!

A girl goes to confession. 'Father,' she says. **'Last night my boyfriend made love to me six times.'** The priest replies, **'For this act of fornication, you must go home and suck six lemons.'** 'And will that absolve me, **Father?'** replies the girl. **'No,'** says the priest. **'But it might wipe that bloody grin off your face.'**

If you're planning on getting married, you might as well go for a younger man – they never mature anyway.

A woman drives her date out into the countryside where they park in a quiet lane. They start to make-out like crazy, but suddenly the guy says, 'Look, I should have mentioned this earlier – but I'm actually a gigolo. I charge £200 for sex.' The woman is stunned, but the guy is gorgeous so she pays up and they bonk each other's brains out. After they've finished, the guy asks to be driven home. The woman asks for her fare. 'What d'you mean, fare?' says the guy. 'Well, I should have mentioned this earlier,' replies the woman. 'But I'm actually a taxi driver. The fare back to town is £200!'

It's a summer night and a couple are out bonking on the garden lawn. **The guy is giving his girlfriend oral sex**. **'I'd love to be able to see this,'** he says. **'I wish I'd bought a torch' 'So do I,'** replies the girl. **'For the last five minutes you've been eating grass!'**

A man goes into a store to buy some condoms. He sees a new brand of multisize condoms, but **isn't sure what size** will fit him. He asks the girl serving behind the counter for some help. 'Are you that big?' asks the girl, holding up **one finger**. 'I'm bigger than that,' says the man. The girl holds up **two fingers**. 'Are you that big?' she asks. 'Bigger,' replies the man. The girl holds up **three fingers**. 'Are you that big?' she asks. 'Well, yes,' says the man. 'I suppose so.' **The girl sticks the three fingers in her mouth and wiggles them around for a bit**. She takes them out and says, **'OK. You're a medium.'**

Agirl and four of her friends go
out shopping. They spend all
day in the mall then get into the
girl's car to go home. Suddenly the
girl remembers she forgot to buy
some condoms. Her boyfriend is
coming home after a trip away so
she'll be needing them. She hurries
to the nearest chemist's,
grabs a packet of

condoms, then finds there's a huge queue at the checkout. She runs to the head of the queue, hands over the condoms and says, 'Do you mind if I butt in and buy these? Only I've got four people waiting in my car...'

What do you call a woman who's allergic to latex?

Mummy.

A woman phones her doctor in the middle of the night. 'Doctor! Doctor! Come quickly,' she says. 'My son has just swallowed a condom!' The doctor gets out of bed and starts pulling on his clothes. The phone rings again – it's the woman. 'It's okay,' she says. 'You don't have to come after all. My husband's just found another one.'

The World's Shortest Fairy Story: Once-upon-a-time a girl said to a man, **'Marry me?'** The man said, **'No.' And the girl went shopping whenever she liked, went out when she wanted, always had a neat house, never had to cook, stayed thin and lived happily ever after.**